Tague, Rachell & the
girls

Z

10 places to eat
TOKYO
東京

"Less is More"

A guide to 10 places serving exceptional traditional food, for the business traveller and leisure traveller wanting to try something different.

By Tagore Ramoutar

www.10placestoeat.com

First Published in 2011.
Published by Longshot Ventures Ltd, UK.

Paperback edition printed in the USA: ISDN 978-1-907837-32-6
Hardback edition printed in the UK: ISDN 978-1-907837-37-1
eBook edition: ISDN 978-1-907837-33-3

10 places to eat guides
Inspiration and Concept

The inspiration behind 10 places to eat was the frustration of travelling on business and being brought to very nice international or French restaurants no matter which country in the world I was in. Even where the food was nominally local it wasn't really traditional food. When I visited Japan, which I went to regularly for three years, I had the freedom to choose and I typically went to little local restaurants who served one type of food very well.

Most guide books overwhelm the reader with choice, and it is difficult to make a decision. This book is based on the premise that most visitors to a city, whether on business or leisure, rarely visit for more than a week, and therefore only need a few choices. This book collects together a very personal view of restaurant recommendations for Tokyo. It is especially relevant for those interested in exploring typical Japanese food served in traditional settings.

When most people think of Japanese food they think of sushi, however in getting to know Japan I have found a wide and varied cuisine with exceptional meat dishes. I originally thought of calling the book the "Meat Lover's Guide to Tokyo", however I have relented and included some fish recommendations.

The recommendations have been visited and sampled by myself as a paying customer. Some of these restaurants have been visited many times and retain a firm place in my heart and memories. Some are well known, others not. All are long established and are generally not trendy and or run by well known chefs. Typically their menus don't really change from year to year, though some will vary by season or catch. Many are not typical business restaurants and are not really suitable at all for business meals (these will be highlighted).

The book and the recommendations are not meant to be comprehensive rather reflect the areas that I have spent most time and my tastes. I hope you can also enjoy them as much as I have.

Introduction to 10 places to eat TOKYO

Tokyo is a city full of restaurants, with a bewildering choice and unbelievable quality. The sheer range of restaurants in any given area often surpasses the range you would find in an entire city in other countries. Many restaurants specialize in a single cuisine and the quality of the ingredients are of paramount importance. For western visitors the restaurant experience can initially seem impossible, with the language, choice, customs and price all proving hard to comprehend.

The Tokyo guide tries to simplify the whole experience by recommending 10 places to experience traditional Japanese food. Each place selected will give you the chance to experience traditional food in an welcoming traditional environment. There are multitude of different types of food to experience and it was difficult to choose just ten. To select only ten, I have focused on simple meals that I think a western visitor might like to experience and will feel comfortable eating alone or with a friend.

I have selected restaurants that focus on one type of food. All the places selected are established businesses with a longstanding reputation and could be considered amongst the best in the genre. The focus of the guide is to give the visitor a taste of local food. It does not seek to rank the different types or select the latest in-restaurant. Places selected have both excellent food and an authentic traditional atmosphere. In many of the places the menu does not change so a recommended meal has been selected. Note prices were correct in January 2011.

The guide gives a history / background of the venue and type of food, a recommended menu and a walking map to get there from the nearest Metro Station. I have included the original Japanese words for the dishes plus phonetic western versions and translations to make it easier for the traveller to use the menus and order even if they are alone. Where helpful I have included tips of how to eat the dish and background to key ingredients. As English is not widely spoken I have also included in the introduction a page of simple phrases useful when going to a restaurant .

Introduction Cont'd

The Tokyo Guide covers most of the main well known traditional food dishes but introduces some that may not be so well known in the west. I have purposefully chosen a representation of meat dishes and fish dishes that the average western visitor might like and are my favourites. See over for the recommended dishes and venues.

The choice of restaurants includes Tokyo's oldest. I have also tried to include recommendations from different areas of central Tokyo to give the visitor a chance to explore. For the purposes of this guide I have defined central Tokyo as within (or close to) the boundaries of the circular JR Yamanote railway line. See over for a simplified map of Tokyo showing where the restaurants are.

HOW TO GET AROUND

Getting around Tokyo can be difficult for first time users. The address system is opaque and difficult to understand. You have two choices: taxis which are ubiquitous and the Metro which is excellent and extensive.

If you are using a taxi make sure you have a printed copy of the address or a map (of where you are going), also ensure it is in Japanese . Unless fluent or very good at pronunciation a map and the address are the only ways of ensuring you get to the right restaurant. Your hotel concierge can print a Japanese map for you.

The Metro is excellent, clean, safe, runs on time and cheap for Tokyo. Whilst first time visitors can find peak time travel difficult due to the shear number of travellers, at other times it is very easy to use if you are already familiar with underground / metro systems. You can pick up a Metro map at your Hotel. There are also excellent guides and maps available on the Metro's website
(http://www.tokyometro.jp/en/index.html)

Note: The maps included in the guide are in English and are designed to help you find the restaurant, where appropriate they include the exit number of the Metro exit closest to the restaurant.

10 meals to eat
10 places to eat

Unagi at Nodaiwa , Higashi-Azabu

Sushi and Sashimi at Tsukiji Sushi-sei
(next to Tsukiji Fish market)

Yakitori at Birdland, Ginza

Tempura at Ten Ichi, Ginza

Soba noodles at Akasaka Takegami,
Akasaka

Ramen noodles at Menya Musashi,
Shinjuku

Tonkatsu at Tonki, Meguro

Shabu-Shabu at Zakuro, Akasaka

Teppanyaki at Ginza Okahan Honten,
Ginza

Katsu karē at the Grill Swiss, Ginza

The Locations of the Recommendations
Central Tokyo

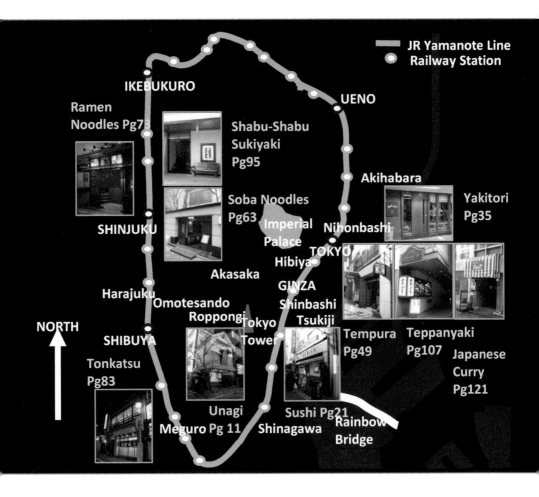

JR Yamanote Line
Railway Station

IKEBUKURO

UENO

Ramen
Noodles Pg73

Shabu-Shabu
Sukiyaki
Pg95

Akihabara

Yakitori
Pg35

Soba Noodles
Pg63

Imperial
Palace

Nihonbashi

SHINJUKU

TOKYO

Hibiya

Akasaka

GINZA

Harajuku

Shinbashi

Omotesando

Tsukiji

Roppongi

Tokyo
Tower

Tempura
Pg49

Teppanyaki
Pg107

NORTH

SHIBUYA

Japanese
Curry
Pg121

Tonkatsu
Pg83

Unagi

Meguro Pg 11

Sushi Pg21

Shinagawa

Rainbow
Bridge

Going to a Restaurant

Going to a restaurant in Japan is a wonderful experience, service is generally excellent though etiquette can seem bewildering. I have tried to give some basic guidance, though as a foreigner you are given much leeway.

Not many restaurants have English speaking staff, though some do have English menus and/or photo menus. However, waiters and waitresses are generally very patient and you will be able to order using the phrases and photos in this book.

On the next page is a simple guide to phrases that may be used in going to a restaurant. It is not a replacement for a good language phrase book but might help. When pronouncing words I have found that splitting the words into pairs of letters (or occasionally trios) when pronouncing tends to make the words understandable. Good luck.

First opening hours. Lunch times are pretty standard from 11.30 to 14.00. However dinner is usually early, some restaurants outside the main centres will close by 20.00, generally after 21.30 it is difficult to find places open. If eating late try near main railway stations and look out for Ramen Noodle restaurants. Traditional restaurants usually hang a half curtain (called a noren) over the entrance, this announces the name, cuisine and also signifies that the restaurant is open.

In many restaurants there are two choices of places to eat, either at the counter or in a private room. At the counter you can usually see your food being prepared and you will sit on stools or chairs. In private rooms you will typically sit on cushions on a tatami matt and have a low table (note you need to take your shoes off before entering the room).

When you walk in you will be greeted by the phrase "Irasshaimase", once seated you will get a fresh damp towel to wipe your hands (hot in the winter and cold in the Summer). Most restaurants specialise in one type of food and choice will be limited, typically there will be set menus, if you are by yourself and speak no Japanese these are a safe bet.

Most traditional meals are eaten with chopsticks. Finally there is no need to tip in Japan, a service charge is added to your bill.

Key Phrases

Basic phrases:	.... arimasu-ka	"Do you have .... ?"
	.... kudasai	"Please give me .... "
	Doomo arigatoo	"Thank you"
	Eigo no menyu ga, arimasu-ka	"Is there a menu in English?"
	Tabe-tai	"I want to try/eat"
	Kaunta wa, aite imasu ka	"Is the counter available?"
	Gochisoo-sama	"thank you for the meal"
	Onegai-shimasu. Gochisoosama	"I'd like to pay now.I had a nice meal"
	Okan'joo	"bill please"
Phrases you may hear:	Go yoyaku-desu-ka?	"Do you have a reservation?"
	Hai. .... De yoyaku shite imasu	"Yes in the name of ...."
	Nan-ni nasaimasu-ka	"What would you like to have?"
	Shokken-o omotome-kudasai	"Please buy meal tickets first"
Key words:	Hai	"yes"
	Iie	"No"
	Menyu	"menu"
	Mizu	"water"
	Biiru	"beer"
	nama biiru	"draft beer"
	Ocha	"Japanese tea"
	Oishii	"tasty/ delicious"
	Sayonara	"goodbye"

Unagi (Grilled Eel)
うなぎ
Nodaiwa

Unagi (Grilled Eel) うなぎ
Background

Unagi is the Japanese word for freshwater eels, the eating of which is very popular in Japan. Eels are found throughout the world, however only in Japan have they become so entwined with the country's culture. Unagi is prized for its flavour and stamina giving properties. Whilst it is eaten all year round, it is traditionally eaten during the summer, particularly at midsummer. Eels are one of the oldest Japanese dishes; the earliest recorded mention dates from 313-759 and is found in a collection of poems called "Manyo-shu".

The original recipe called gamayaki was simply skewered eel grilled over a fire. By the Edo period (1603 to 1868) unagi was eaten by the nobility and soya sauce added to the grilled eel (the dish was called kabayaki). At the end of the Edo period the founder of Nodaiwa (Noda Iwajiro) created his sauce, which is still used today. Noda Iwajiro's "taré" (sauce) is made from soya sauce, mirin (mild saké) and other ingredients that are still secret today. Grilled eel without sauce is called shirayaki, and when served as part of a set meal the meal will include a clear eel liver soup called kimosui.

Cooking of good unagi requires highly skilled cooks and recipes for the tare sauce tend to be closely guarded secrets. Unagi in Tokyo is cut into fillets and grilled over hot charcoal and then steamed to remove excess fat, the tare is added and then the unagi grilled a second time. Good unagi is tender and soft inside and crispy/ grilled almost caramelized on the outside.

Eel numbers in the wild are falling but it is not known why. Found in ponds and rivers, eels grow for between 6-12 years for males and 10-20 years for females before travelling vast distances to spawn and then die. Natural eels are the most prized for their taste and should always be served fresh to keep it's softness. Eels are delivered and kept alive in tanks; in good restaurants the eels are killed and cut into fillets only when the customer orders.

Nodaiwa
Azabu

Nodaiwa
Azabu

Nodaiwa Azabu
1-5-4, Higashiazabu, Minato-ku, Tokyo
Tel : +81 (0)3 3583 7852

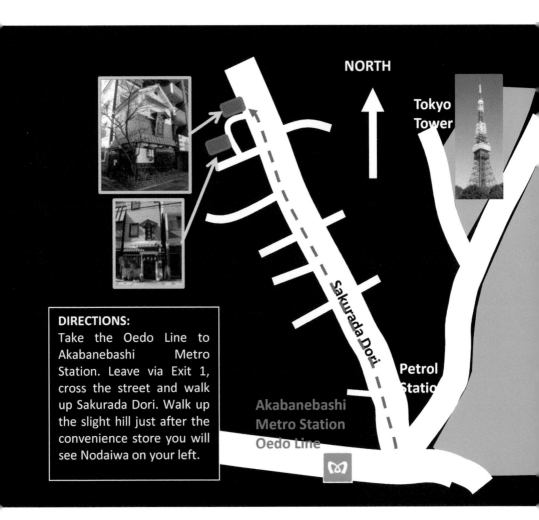

NORTH

Tokyo Tower

Sakurada Dori

Petrol Station

Akabanebashi Metro Station Oedo Line

DIRECTIONS:
Take the Oedo Line to Akabanebashi Metro Station. Leave via Exit 1, cross the street and walk up Sakurada Dori. Walk up the slight hill just after the convenience store you will see Nodaiwa on your left.

Open daily (except Sundays)
Lunch   11.00–13.30
Dinner   17.00–20.00

Nodaiwa
Background and Recommended Meal

Nodaiwa is one of the most famous places to experience Unagi (grilled Eel) in Japan. Nodiawa is over 160 years old and has been managed for five generations by the same family. Nodaiwa is one of the few restaurants still specialising in natural fresh water eels (these are caught from Mid-April to December). In 1996 Nodaiwa opened a branch in Paris and in 2010 the original restaurant in Azabu was awarded one Michelin Star.

Nodaiwa is located on Sakurada-dori in the quiet area of Azabu in the lee of Tokyo Tower. The main building - a small, rustic kura (storehouse) situated in the middle of the city, is 160 years old. The rooms have bamboo ceiling and dark wooden beams and service is immaculately carried out by kimono dressed ladies.

Although Nodaiwa is relatively expensive for unagi, it is without doubt the best place to experience it for the first time, as both the food and dining experience are great.

If the main restaurant is busy you will be escorted to their sister restaurant close by, see the pictures overleaf. Here the ambience is just as traditional and the service exquisite. Note Nodaiwa does have English menus that are available on request.

In terms of a recommended meal, I have been cautious and recommended the set meal that this restaurant is most famous for - the Shirayaki Meal. For lunch, the Shirayaki Set Menu, including Green Tea, costs 3,520 yen. The Shirayaki Menu consists of a metal box with unflavored delicately cooked eel (crispy on the outside and creamy inside) with salt, soy sauce and wasabi to taste. It is accompanied by sides dishes of steamed rice, eel liver soup (the clear soup has fresh mitsuba leaves and eel liver in a clear broth - and should be sipped from the bowl), pickled vegetables and grated daikon.

Note: at Nodaiwa you pay at the table and they take credit cards.

Shirayaki Set Menu
Nodaiwa

Nodaiwa Annexe
Azabu

Nodaiwa Annexe
Azabu

Sushi
寿司 or 鮨
Tsukiji Sushi Sei Honten

Sushi寿司or 鮨
Background

Sushi is without doubt the most famous Japanese food and is now widely available outside Japan, but to taste it in Japan is an entirely different experience. Freshness is key for good sushi, therefore many connoisseurs eat it as early in the morning as possible and eating sushi early in the morning in Tsukiji Market is the ultimate sushi experience.

Sushi is one of Japan's earliest types of food, the oldest record of sushi appears in 718 in the Yōrō Code (a governing document). This type of sushi was called narezushi and consisted of fermented fish and rice, preserved with salt. This fermented fish had a very pungent smell and only the fish was eaten with the rice thrown away. In fact sushi originally meant "it's sour" in an ancient form of Japanese.

Sushi slowly evolved over next 800 years, the rice began to be boiled rather than steamed and rice vinegar invented. By the late 1500s vinegar began to be used and the rice eaten rather than thrown away. The addition of vinegar to the rice led the abandonment of fermentation.

Modern sushi was created by Hanaya Yohei during the first half of the 19th century in Tokyo (then called Edo). This sushi was fast food prepared quickly with fresh ingredients and eaten with one's hands. It consisted of hand formed sushi with vinegared rice topped with fish or seafood*. This sushi was known as Edomae zushi because it used fresh fish from Edo-mae (Edo Bay). Even today it is still formally known as Edomae nigirizushi and this is the form we generally know and eat today. Nigirizushi was an instant hit and it spread rapidly through Edo, within 20 years the number of sushi restaurants in Edo numbered in the thousands.

---

* raw fish by itself is called sashimi

Tsukiji Sushi Sei Honten
Tsukiji

Tsukiji Sushi Sei Honten
Tsukiji

Tsukiji Sushi Sei Honten
4-13-9 Tsukiji
Tel: +81(0)3 3541 7720

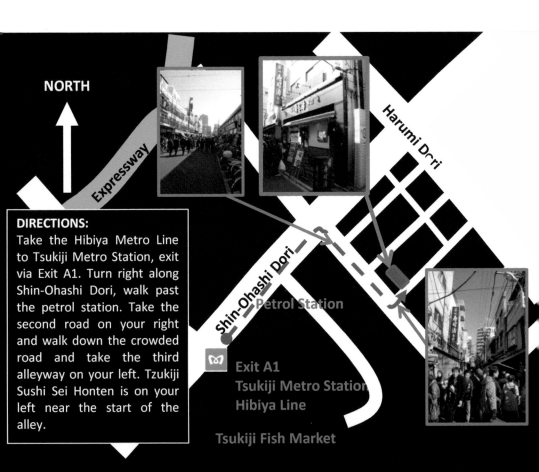

NORTH

Expressway

Harumi Dori

Shin-Ohashi Dori

DIRECTIONS:
Take the Hibiya Metro Line to Tsukiji Metro Station, exit via Exit A1. Turn right along Shin-Ohashi Dori, walk past the petrol station. Take the second road on your right and walk down the crowded road and take the third alleyway on your left. Tzukiji Sushi Sei Honten is on your left near the start of the alley.

Petrol Station

Exit A1
Tsukiji Metro Station
Hibiya Line

Tsukiji Fish Market

Open daily (except Sundays and National holidays)
Mon-Fri   8.30-14.00,   Dinner 17.00-20:30
Sat   8.00-10.30pm
Sun   Closed

It has space for 8 at tables, and 29 at the counter.
Credit cards are accepted

Sushi at Tsukiji Sushi Sei Honten
Background and Recommended Menu

Tsukiji Sushi Sei is located in the outer section of the Central Wholesale Fish Market Tsukiji. Tsukiji Fish Market is the largest fish market in the world handing over 2000 metric tonnes per day. The market was relocated to Tsukiji from Nihonbashi after the Great Kanto earthquake of 1923 and the huge current facility dates from 1935. It is definitely worth an early morning visit to see the auctions (note the auctions finish by 7.00 and activity ramps down from 11.00).

Tsukiji Sushi Sei's original restaurant opened in 1889. This location is the main branch restaurant of Sushi Sei, a chain which now has more than twenty restaurants in Japan. This restaurant serves wonderfully fresh sushi in the edomaezuchi style and has great counter seats for watching the sushi being prepared. Often there is a queue but it is definitely worth the wait. Whilst no English is spoken this restaurant really works for foreigners, with a great laminated card menu (see next page) meaning it is easy to order a-la-carte. Alternatively their set menus allow you to relax and try all the main types.

I recommend the Takumi menu for 2,500 yen accompanied by sake (this will be additional cost), again you get a laminated card showing what you will get, taking all the pressure out of ordering. It is place you can visit by yourself even if you don't speak Japanese. Note: It is only really suitable for small parties of 1-4 otherwise you are unlikely to get a seat or might have to wait a long time. When you have finished you pay at the small counter near the door.

お好み握り
Sushi a la Carte (one piece)

Some sushi are not available in certain seasons.

赤身 210yen
Lean tuna
金槍魚
살고기

中とろ 370yen
Medium Fatty Tuna
金槍魚濃味美的中膜部
쥰토로(다랑어 살이 지방이 많은 부분)

大とろ 530yen
Fatty tuna
金槍魚的脂肪多的部分
대토로(다랑어 살의 지방이 많은 부분)

サーモン 160yen
Salmon
鮭魚
연어

鯛 160yen
Red snapper
真鯛
도이

平目 320yen
Fluke
鮃
히라메

ぶり 320yen
Yellowtail
鰤
지랄해

いか 270yen
Squid
墨魚
물오징어

生たこ 210yen
Octpus
章魚
연

いわし 210yen
Sardine
沙丁魚
정어리

あじ 210yen
Japanese mackerel
料魚
전갱이

鯖 210yen
Mackerel
鯖魚
고등어

とびこ 160yen
Flying fish roe
飛魚子
소리개근

白魚 320yen
White bait
銀魚
뱅어

鰹 270yen
Bonito
鰹魚
가다랭이

穴子 270yen
Japanese sea eel
星鰻
붕장어

玉子 160yen
Egg
玉子
게란쌀

お好み握り
Sushi a la Carte (one piece)

Some sushi are not available in certain seasons.

ぼたんえび 420yen
Botan shrimp
牡丹蝦
게란새

車海老 530yen
Japanese shrimp
対虾
참새우

ずわい蟹(茹で) 420yen
Boilled snow crab
堪察加拟石蟹（煮）
바다침게 (대처)

ほたて貝 210yen
Scallop
帆貝
이삭 새로 조개

青柳 370yen
Orange clam
马珂肉
파룻파룻한 버들

赤貝 420yen
Red clam
蚶子
새고막

みる貝 530yen
Giant clam
西施舌
보는 조개

あわび 630yen
Ahalone
鮑魚
전복

生うに 630yen
Sea urchin
海胆
순 (솥) 섬게

いくら 420yen
Salmon roe
鮭魚子
아우리

  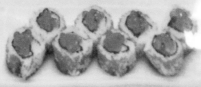

かっぱ巻 420yen
cucumber roll
黄瓜巻
갓빠 컨

鉄火巻 740yen
Tuna roll
金槍魚巻
철화권

サーモンスキンロール 1,260yen
Salmon skin roll
鮭魚皮巻
사몬스킨롤

Cutting Tuna
Tsukiji Sushi Sei Honten

Grating Fresh Wasabi
Tsukiji Sushi Sei Honten

Lean Tuna, Medium Fatty and Red Snapper Edomaezushi
Tsukiji Sushi Sei Honten

Edomaezushi
Tsukiji Sushi Sei Honten

Edomaezushi
Tsukiji Sushi Sei Honten

Uragasumi Sake
Tsukiji Sushi Sei Honten

Yakitori
焼き鳥or やきとり
Birdland

Yakitori 焼き鳥orやきとり
Background

Yakitori is the ultimate Japanese fast food, often consumed with a beer by salary men before their long commute home. Yakitori is charcoal grilled chicken on a skewer. Generally it is several bite-sized pieces of chicken meat, or chicken offal, skewered on a bamboo skewer, though you also get some other dishes including vegetables. It usually comes either with salt or with tare sauce, which is generally made up of mirin*, sake, soy sauce and sugar. The barbeque sauce is applied to the skewered meat and is grilled over charcoal until delicately cooked. The quality of the yakitori is driven by the quality of the tare and the charcoal.

Common dishes are:

toriniku - all white meat on skewer
tsukune (つくね) - chicken meatballs
tebasaki (手羽先) - chicken wing
bonjiri (ぼんじり) - chicken tail
nankotsu (なんこつ) - chicken cartilage
shiro (シロ) - chicken small intestines
gyūtan (牛タン) - thinly sliced ox tongue,
rebā (レバー) - chicken liver
(tori)kawa (とり)かわ) - crispy chicken skin
hatsu (ハツ) or kokoro (こころ) - chicken heart
sunagimo (砂肝) or zuri (ずり) - chicken gizzard

Yakitori restaurants are often little more than counters with a few stools. Yakitori restaurants usually have a small red lantern outside with the character for tori or bird (鳥) or the full Yakitori やきとり. Whilst the rough and ready counter walk-in yakitori places are great fun they are difficult to visit without a fluent Japanese speaker. Birdland has been chosen as a place where you can experience yakitori in a more familiar restaurant setting, the menu is available in English and it is renown for great high quality yakitori.

---

* Mirin is sweet mild sake used in cooking.

Birdland
Ginza

Birdland
Ginza

Birdland
Tsukamoto Sozan Bldg B1F, Ginza 4-2-15
Tel: +81 (0)3 5250 1081

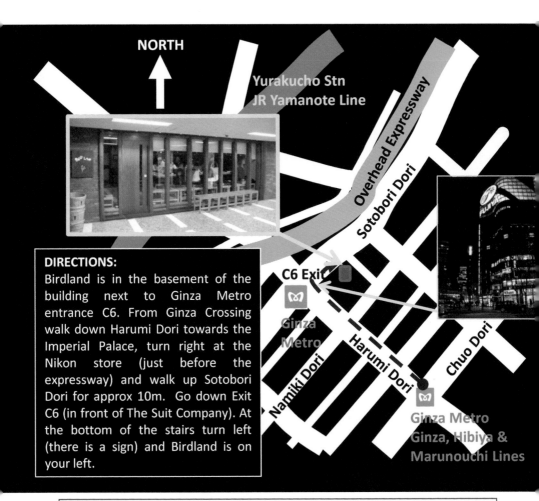

NORTH

Yurakucho Stn
JR Yamanote Line

Overhead Expressway

Sotobori Dori

C6 Exit

Ginza Metro

Namiki Dori

Harumi Dori

Chuo Dori

Ginza Metro
Ginza, Hibiya &
Marunouchi Lines

DIRECTIONS:

Birdland is in the basement of the building next to Ginza Metro entrance C6. From Ginza Crossing walk down Harumi Dori towards the Imperial Palace, turn right at the Nikon store (just before the expressway) and walk up Sotobori Dori for approx 10m. Go down Exit C6 (in front of The Suit Company). At the bottom of the stairs turn left (there is a sign) and Birdland is on your left.

Opening hours (five days a week. Closed: Mondays, Sundays and public holidays)

Dinner Only   17.00-21.30

Dress: casual. Suitable for guests.

Reservations are essential as it can get very busy. Whilst the website is Japanese there is a reservation section in English.

http://www.opentable.jp/en-GB/rest_profile.aspx?rid=10955&restref=10955

Birdland
Ginza

Birdland
Background and Recommended Menu

Birdland is located in the heart of Ginza and is considered one of the best yakitori restaurants in Tokyo, in 2010 it achieved a Michelin Star. Birdland was first set up in 1987 out in Asagaya (a suburb of Tokyo) but moved to Ginza. Located in the basement near the exit of the Metro Station, Birdland is an unassuming place, but once inside it is full of atmosphere. If you can, sit at the counter where you will be able to see the yakitori being cooked in front of you and soak up the atmosphere.

Birdland's yakitori is relatively modern and focuses on flavours with many types using sansho pepper (Sichuan pepper) which creates a tingly numbness. Birdland does have an English menu and it is possible to create your own meal ordering individual items, however to experience yakitori more fully I recommend trying one of the set menus which will take you through the tastes and different types of yakitori. I recommend the 6,000 yen menu.

The menu is served as individual skewers of yakitori with the next one only being served once the current one is complete. You can eat directly from the skewer but more typically the meat is taken off the skewer and then eaten with chopsticks, the finished skewer should be placed in the container in front of you.

The 6,000 yen menu includes multiple skewers followed by oyakodon (chicken and egg over rice). The skewers are: white meat chicken with wasabi, chicken hearts, crispy skin, tofu, ginnan fruit, chicken kidneys, chicken balls, chicken thighs with skin (off the skewer) and sansho pepper, mushrooms, chicken and spring onion.

Draft beer is the recommended accompaniment with yakitori, though Birdland also has a good wine selection.

Cost of the meal including drinks is approximately 9,350 yen.

BIRD LAND

White Chicken Yakitori
Birdland

Chicken Balls Yakitori
Birdland

Chicken Yakitori
Birdland

Chicken Yakitori off the Skewer
Birdland

Oyakodon (Chicken and Egg over Rice)
Birdland

Tempura
天ぷら
Ten-Ichi
天一

Tempura 天ぷら or 天麩羅
Background

Tempura is simply battered deep fried seafood or vegetables, though this description hardly does justice to this most Japanese of dishes. Good tempura is a light delicate meal.

Tempura actually has its roots in a Portuguese cooking style (peixinhos da horta) introduced by Portuguese missionaries and traders in the middle of the 16th century. Reputedly tempura was loved by the first shogun* of the Tokugawa Shogunate. By the end of the 19th century tempura had become a popular fast food bought from stalls and pushcarts through out Tokyo. Nowadays tempura is available from fast food chains to top restaurants.

The key to good tempura is fresh ingredients, presentation and a skilled chef and great batter. Tempura batter is very light and is made from cold water (some chefs use sparkling water), eggs and flour. Usually it is roughly mixed in small quantities using chopsticks; mixing only takes a few seconds and batter is lumpy and cold, which helps to give crisp tempura when cooked. The vegetables and seafood are often thinly sliced and dipped quickly to give a thin transparent coating of batter before frying one at a time in sesame oil or a combination of vegetable and sesame oils; the oil is kept at between 160°C and 180 °C. Food is cooked quickly sometimes for as little as a few seconds.

Tempura can be ordered individually but usually is ordered as a set meal (teishoku). Tempura is served piece by piece as it is cooked. It is best eaten hot and eaten with a dipping sauce or salt.

_____

* Shoguns were the hereditary military leaders who ruled Japan in the name of the Emperor from the 12th Century until 1867.

Ten-Ichi
Ginza

Ten-Ichi
Ginza

Ten-Ichi
Namiki Dori 6-6-5 Ginza
Tel: +81 (0)3 3571 1272

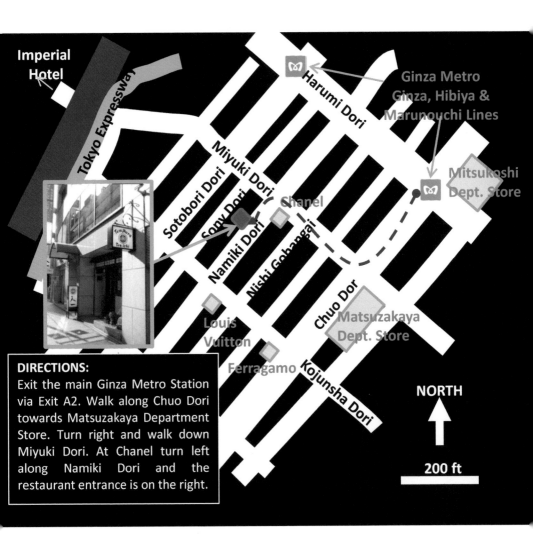

Imperial Hotel

Tokyo Expressway

Harumi Dori

Ginza Metro
Ginza, Hibiya &
Marunouchi Lines

Miyuki Dori

Sotobori Dori

Sony Dori

Chanel

Mitsukoshi
Dept. Store

Namiki Dori

Nishi Gobangai

Chuo Dori

Louis Vuitton

Matsuzakaya
Dept. Store

Ferragamo

Kojunsha Dori

NORTH

200 ft

DIRECTIONS:
Exit the main Ginza Metro Station via Exit A2. Walk along Chuo Dori towards Matsuzakaya Department Store. Turn right and walk down Miyuki Dori. At Chanel turn left along Namiki Dori and the restaurant entrance is on the right.

Open seven days a week:

Open   11.30-21.30 (Last Orders)

Takes credit cards and is suitable for business meals.

Ten-Ichi
Background and Recommended Menu

Ten-Ichi is probably the most famous and recognised restaurant for tempura. Originally established in 1930, it is now a chain of over 20 restaurants. The main branch of this restaurant is located on Namiki Dori, famous for its luxury brands and bars, in the heart of Ginza. Over the years it has hosted many famous foreign visitors, the pictures of some of them are featured in the reception area.

Once inside the restaurant is laid out in a traditional Japanese wooden style, with a large counter in the basement where one can watch the tempura being made by the white clad chefs. On entering you are brought to seat by a kimono clad waitress, on placing your order a white bib is tied on you and then it is time to sit back and enjoy the show.

The batter is made at the counter in a beautiful ceramic pot and each selected ingredient dipped and fried in front of you. Each piece is cooked individually for you and the meal is paced by the process of cooking. The set menus tend to start with prawns and fish then move on to the vegetables and finishing again with fish. Tempura is eaten hot using chopsticks, each piece is usually dipped either in a sauce with diakon* or in lemon juice with a pinch of salt.

The recommended meal is a set menu, this one is a lunch one but there are dinner ones also (note: evening menus are more expensive). I recommend the Hana Menu costing 8,400 yen for this you get two prawn tempura, two fish, three vegetable (the type will vary by season) a piece of conger eel tempura and kakiage, a kind of shrimp patty in batter. In addition you get salad, rice and miso soup. To drink I would recommend saki, which is served in a beautiful ceramic cup/ flat jug, though tempura works well with beer also.

If you visit at lunch on a weekend there is no need to book, at all other times you need to book; to get the full experience book a counter seat.

---

* Daikon is a giant white radish

Tempura
Ten-Ichi

Ebi Tempura
Ten-Ichi

Asparagus Tempura
Ten-Ichi

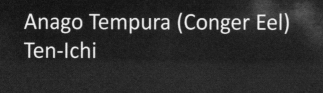

Anago Tempura (Conger Eel)
Ten-Ichi

Shrimp Patty
Ten-Ichi

Sake
Ten-Ichi

Tempura Batter Bowl
Ten-Ichi

Soba Noodles
そば or 蕎麦
Akasaka Takegami
たけがみ

Soba Noodles そば or 蕎麦
Background

Noodles are one of the main types of Japanese food, though less well known outside Japan than sushi. There are three main types: ramen noodles (see separate section) soba noodles and udon noodles. I have chosen soba noodles as they are more popular in Tokyo; udon noodles are more popular in Kansai (the region including Osaka and Kyoto).

Soba noodles are thin noodles made from buckwheat, often served cold in the summer and hot in the winter in a soup. When served cold they are presented on a bamboo screen in a lacquer box and served with a dipping sauce, this style is called mori-soba. Hot noodles are served in a bowl of hot broth, and are slurped noisily from the bowl, this style of noodles is called kake-soba. The slurping noise is traditional and is done to help cool the noodles.

Soba is the noodle most closely associated with Tokyo and still the most popular. Its roots are in the Tokugawa or Edo period (1603-1868) when its consumption grew popular with the people of Edo (Tokyo) as it prevented beri-beri*, a disease that had become common due to rising consumption of white rice. Most neighbourhoods had at least one soba outlet and these would function as a local café and bar serving sake. Still today there are many neighbourhood soba outlets; and soba noodle restaurants run from inexpensive fast food outlets in train stations through to formal kaiseki style restaurants. **

I have chosen a more formal kaiseki style soba restaurant called Akasaka Takegami whose owner is renown for his soba.

---

* Buckwheat soba is rich in thiamine which helps to prevent beri-beri.

** Kaiseki is a traditional formal multi course Japanese meal.

Akasaka Takegami

Akasaka
Takegami

Akasaka Takegami
Net Akasaka Build. 1F, 3-13-16 Akasaka
Tel: +81 (0)3 3586 3636

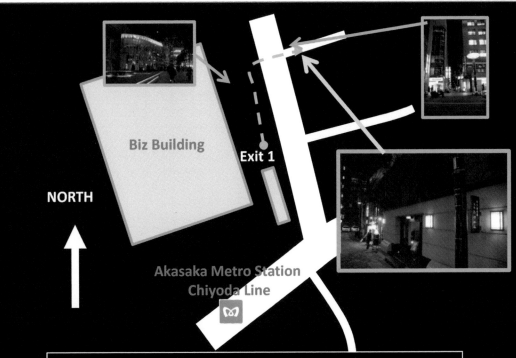

NORTH

Biz Building

Exit 1

Akasaka Metro Station
Chiyoda Line

DIRECTIONS:
Take the Chiyoda Metro line to Akasaka station. Exit the station via Exit 1, as you come up the escalators you will see a sign for Maxims in the 2F window of the building in front of you. Walk towards Maxims, you will see a docomo shop on your right (on the opposite side of the road) with a pedestrianized lane on its right-hand side. Cross the road and walk down the lane, the restaurant is about 10m down on your right.

Open six days a week (closed on Sun and National holidays):
Lunch: 11.30-15.00 (14.30 Last Orders)
Dinner   17.30-22.00 (21.30 Last Orders)

English menu available. Suitable for business meals
http://www.kamiya-m.com/akasaka/ (only in Japanese)

Soba-kaiseki at Akasaka Takegami Background and Recommended Menu

Akasaka Takegami is an elegant restaurant located in the heart of Akasaka, an area well known for restaurants. Established in 1998, Akasaka Takegami is one of four restaurants run by the chef—owner Kamiya-san.

Akasaka Takegami is a modern Ryotei* and is known for its handmade soba and more formal soba-kaiseki meals. Whilst modern inside, Akasaka Takegami has a traditional layout and style, with private rooms and formal dining. In addition to the formal private rooms it has an enclosed private counter space with seating for nine, where guests can see food being prepared. There is also an area for making the soba that is visible in the reception area. It is recommended that you book the counter space.

Kaiseki is a traditional formal multi-course Japanese dinner. The courses tend to small and beautifully presented. Kaiseki typically consists of an appetizer, sashimi, a simmered dish, a grilled dish, and a steamed course. Note kaiseki tends to be expensive so be careful.

The chosen menu at the Akasaka Takegami is the basic soba-kaiseki set menu costing 5,250 yen called "Aizu" course, it consists of an appetizer followed by six courses. It is recommended that you have a small beer with the appetizer and then move on to sake. The recommended meal is: sakizuke (appetizer); aburi-zushi (sushi, very lightly broiled on top) this can be substituted with sashimi as I have done; followed by arabiki age sobagaki (deep-fried coarse soba dumpling); yakimono (grilled dish of the day), on the day I visited the choice was between Japanese Spanish mackerel teriyaki or seared beef; soba in two different styles, cold (seiro) soba noodles, hot (kake) soba noodles in broth; and finishing with a dessert of mizuyokan (sweet bean jelly) with green tea and sorbet (yuzu and cassis flavours). Note: the restaurant does have an abbreviated lunch menu in English, and some staff speak a little English; in addition they take credit cards.

---

* Ryotei is a traditional high end Japanese restaurant often only accepting new customers if referred by an existing customer (though not in this case).

Arabiki Age Sobagaki (Deep Fried Soba)
Akasaka Takegami

Hot Soba Noodles
Akasaka Takegami

Cold Soba Noodles
Akasaka Takegami

Ramen Noodles
ラーメン
Menya Musashi
麺屋武蔵

Ramen Noodles ラーメン
Background

Ramen noodles are an intrinsic part of modern Japanese culture, even famously featuring in the 1986 film Tampopo. They are immensely popular as everyday food, eaten either at home or in local restaurants. Many of the restaurants stay open late and are popular as an after drinks meal as they are thought to help prevent hangovers.

Originally Chinese in origin, ramen noodles are a noodle dish consisting of Chinese-style wheat noodles served in a meat broth, flavoured with soy sauce or miso, and sliced pork, dried seaweed, kamaboko (sliced fish paste loaf often green in colour) and green onions.

At the turn of the 20th century ramen noodles were only sold in Chinese restaurants. However after the Second World War Japanese restaurants began to sell ramen noodles also. During the next 40 to 50 years many regional variations were created and now many areas of Japan have their own local version.

Ramen are made from wheat flour, salt, water, and kansui (a special type of alkaline mineral water). The kansui gives the noodles a yellowish colour and firm texture. The broth is made from stock combined with a variety of ingredients. There are four general categories:

Shio (salt) is a clear pale light ramen;

Tonkotsu (pork bone) ramen is a hearty creamy white colored broth made from boiling pork bones, fat and collagen;

Shōyu ramen is a brown and clear color broth, based on a chicken and vegetable (or sometimes fish or beef) stock with plenty of soy sauce;

Miso ramen has miso (a salty Japanese seasoning) blended with either an oily chicken or fish broth.

Tokyo style ramen consists of thin slightly curly noodles served in a soy-flavoured chicken broth. The broth is topped with chopped scallion, menma (lactic fermented pickled bamboo shoot), sliced pork, kamaboko, boiled egg, nori (dried seaweed) and spinach.

Menya Musashi
Shinjuku

Menya Musashi
Shinjuku

Menya Musashi
K-1 Build. 1F, 7-2-6 Nishishinjuku
Tel: +81 (0)3 3363 4634

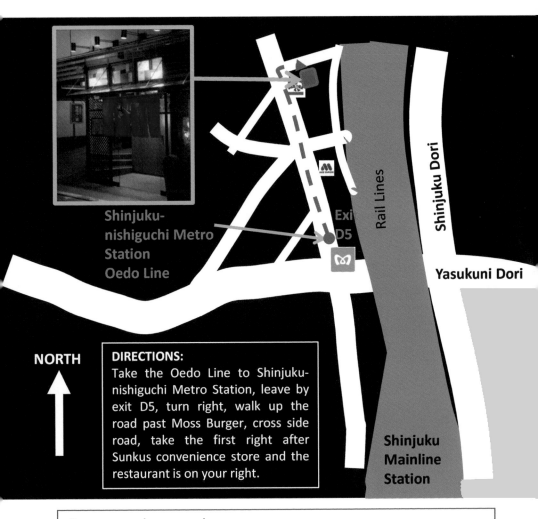

Shinjuku-nishiguchi Metro Station Oedo Line

Exit D5

Rail Lines

Shinjuku Dori

Yasukuni Dori

Shinjuku Mainline Station

NORTH

DIRECTIONS:
Take the Oedo Line to Shinjuku-nishiguchi Metro Station, leave by exit D5, turn right, walk up the road past Moss Burger, cross side road, take the first right after Sunkus convenience store and the restaurant is on your right.

Open seven days a week:
Monday to Saturday. Lunch:	11.30-15.30
Dinner:	16.30-21.30
Sunday	11.30-19.00

Credit cards are not accepted
Only counter seating available. Very casual

Menya Musashi (Shinjuku Branch) Background and Recommended Menu

Established in 1998, Menya Musashi has become famous for its ramen, and often has long queues. Menya Musashi Shinjuku Branch is a small counter based noodle shop with a great atmosphere, coupled with great simple noodles. The pork is very tender, having been stewed for hours in sweet Japanese wine and soy sauce and melts in your mouth. The dishes use great quality noodles to create traditional, quick, simple and hearty ramen dishes. It has nineteen seats looking into the kitchen / preparation area.

The "Musashi" in the name refers to the warrior Miyamoto Musashi, the famed master of double sword style, hence the imagery on the signs. Also look out for the pictures on the stools.

The service is typically modern Japanese with a lot of theatre, the staff are very animated and chant every time the ramen noodles are taken out of the water and drained via a dramatic swinging motion.

Most days you will have to queue, but generally the queue moves very quickly as service is fast and people do not linger. You need to get a ticket from the ordering machine on your left at the top of the stairs prior to sitting down. You hand over the ticket once you are seated; and then choose the strength of the broth and the size of the bowl. Whilst the waiters speak little English they are very helpful.

The recommended dish is Musashi Ramen; to order push the button circled in the picture. Note the dish in the photograph is 900 yen. The ramen is Tokyo style and consists of slightly curly noodles served in a soy-flavoured chicken broth, topped with chopped scallion, menma, sliced pork, kamaboko, egg and nori. The dishes are large so the 900 yen dish is more than adequate however if you want extra pork press the 1000 yen button, then feed in the money. Then sit down and enjoy the cooking theatre and food.

Musashi Ramen Noodles
Menya Musashi

Menya Musashi
Shinjuku

Menya Musashi
Shinjuku

Tonkatsu
豚カツ or とんかつ
Tonki
とんき

Tonkatsu
豚カツ, とんかつ, or トンカツ
Background

Tonkatsu is a type of yōshoku, meaning western-influenced cooking which originated during the Meiji Restoration (from 1868) when Japan was opened to the west and the ban on red meat lifted. Originally called katsuretsu ("cutlet"), or even katsu, early versions were beef. Pork was first served in 1890 in a western restaurant in Ginza and the term "tonkatsu" ("pork katsu") started to be used from the 1930s. Tonkatsu has become the dominant cuisine for pork in Japan, and more than other yōshoku tonkatsu is now very much a Japanese dish. Today tonkatsu is usually served with rice, miso soup and Japanese pickles and eaten with chopsticks.

Tonkatsu consists of slowly deep-fried breaded pork cutlet (one to two centimeters thick) sliced into bite-sized pieces, served with shredded cabbage, rice in a separate bowl and miso soup. The most common cuts are hire (pork fillet ヒレ, a leaner cut with no untrimmed fat) or rōsu (pork loin ロース, with some untrimmed fat). The cooking process of good tonkatsu produces a non-greasy thick crunchy crisp texture on the outside that contrasts with the juicy meat inside. With both cuts the process of preparing does not vary; with the meat being lightly seasoned, lightly coated with flour and then dipped into beaten egg before being coated with panko (breadcrumbs), after which it is deep fried. Tonkatsu is usually eaten with a thick sauce called tonkatsu sōsu (it is made from pureed apples and like a thick Worcestershire sauce, though not so spicy) and yellow karashi (Japanese mustard). The sōsu is put on the pork and usually a thinner version is put on the grated cabbage. The miso soup served often includes pieces of pork and is called tonjiru.

Tonkatsu is generally inexpensive and the quality of the tonkatsu is highly dependent on the quality of the meat and crispness of the breaded exterior. Good tonkatsu is utterly fantastic and an experience not to be missed.

Tonki
Meguro

Tonki
Meguro

Tonki
The Counter View

Tonki
Preparation Area

Tonki
Shimomeguro 1-1-2, Meguro
Tel: +81 (0)3 3491 9928

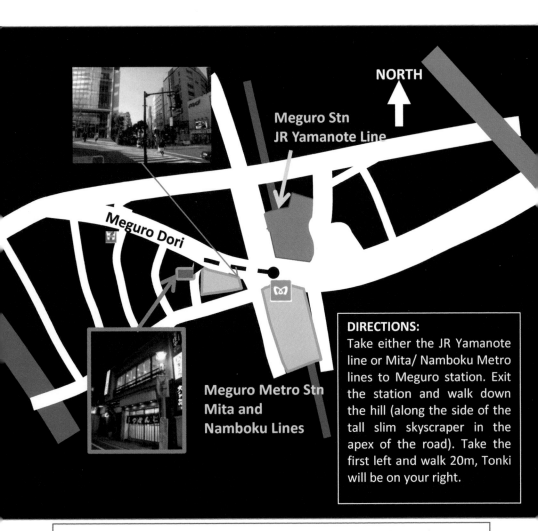

NORTH

Meguro Stn
JR Yamanote Line

Meguro Dori

DIRECTIONS:
Take either the JR Yamanote line or Mita/ Namboku Metro lines to Meguro station. Exit the station and walk down the hill (along the side of the tall slim skyscraper in the apex of the road). Take the first left and walk 20m, Tonki will be on your right.

Meguro Metro Stn
Mita and
Namboku Lines

Open six days a week (Closed at Lunch time and the third Monday every month):

Wednesday to Monday	16.00-22.45
Tuesday	Closed

Note: Does NOT accept credit cards

Tonki
Background and Recommended Menu

Tonki is a Tokyo institution, located in Meguro, it is off the beaten track (though easily accessible from Central Tokyo) and is often overlooked by visitors who go to the more central Maisen restaurant in Omotesando. Believe me it is worth the extra little effort it takes to go to Tonki. Tonki was established over 70 years ago in West Meguro and relocated to its present location in 1967.

Located on a quiet street just down from the train and metro stations, practically the only people walking along the street are going to Tonki.

On entering you enter a warm busy world. On the right hand side sit people waiting for a counter space. In the middle of the room the plain scrubbed wood cooking area is surrounded by the counter and bustling white clad .

When you walk in you are greeted by the maître'd/ kitchen manager who stands behind the counter, he will ask you for your order and then point to an area on the wall where you are to wait for a counter space to come free. He will remember your order and when it is almost ready he will allocate counter seats for you by pointing to where to go. It is an amazing feat of memory and organization which no matter how often you go is impressive. The process of preparation and cooking happens right in front of you, each of the staff specialize in one element of the process: the frying, the slicing, the cabbage etc. Watching the old man cut is like watching poetry in motion, he handles the hot tonkatsu straight from the fryer with his bare hands.

The recommended meal is simply rōsu katsu with a beer. The rōsu katsu will cost 1,800 yen. Tonkatsu at Tonki is an experience not to be missed and almost every time I have visited Japan I have had the privilege of going there. Whilst no English appears to be spoken, there are almost always western faces and it is very welcoming. Just ask for "rōsu katsu".

Tonki
Cutting the Tonkatsu

Tonki
The Fryers

Shabu-Shabu or Sukiyaki
しゃぶしゃぶ or すき焼き
Zakuro
ざくろ 赤坂店

Shabu-Shabu しゃぶしゃぶ
Sukiyaki すき焼き
Background

Nabemono dishes are one pot stews where the ingredients are quickly cooked at the table in a shared pot. Traditionally these were eaten during the winter, though nowadays there are specialist restaurants that serve nabemono all year round. There are many types of nabemono but two related types have become popular and both are well worth experiencing.

Shabu-shabu: thinly sliced beef and other ingredients including shiitake mushrooms and enokitake mushrooms, eaten with a "ponzu" (citrus based sauce) or "goma" (a sesame seed dip). Followed by kishimen (flat noodles) cooked in the leftover broth.

Sukiyaki: thinly sliced beef, tofu, vegetables stewed in sweetened soy and eaten with a raw egg dip and followed by starch noodles cooked in the same sauce. If cooked in the Kanto* style the ingredients are stewed in a pre-prepared mixture of soy sauce, sugar, sake and mirin (in Kansai* style they are mixed at the table). Sukiyaki is popular at bōnenkai, Japanese year-end parties.

Of the two, sukiyaki is the more traditional dish, tracing its origins to medieval times, though it only became available in a recognizable modern form using beef in the 1860s with the opening of Japan to foreigners and with it the increasing use of beef, eggs and milk. Suki means spade in Japanese and yaki broiled, and it is believed that the name comes from the practice of peasants cooking sweet potatoes on their spades in the fields. The first sukiyaki restaurant, Isekuma, opened in Yokohama in 1862.

Shabu-shabu traces its origins to the Chinese hot pot known as "shuan yang rou" and was introduced in Japan in the 20th century with the opening of a shabu-shabu restaurant "Suehiro" in Osaka. The name shabu-shabu coming from the sound made swishing the beef or vegetable in a pot of boiling water, literally shabu-shabu means swish-swish.

---

* Kanto is the region including Tokyo, Kansai is the region including Osaka, Kyoto and Kobe

Zakuro
Akasaka

Zakuro
Akasaka

Zakuro
Background and Recommended Menu

Zakuro Akasaka is a relatively old established restaurant specializing in sukiyaki and shabu-shabu. Established in 1955 it relocated to its present location in Biz Tower in 2007. Zakuro means pomegranate in Japanese. It is a traditional Japanese restaurant in a modern environment and focuses on serving the best Japanese beef. It offers both shabu-shabu, sukiyaki, which are cooked and served at the table by ladies in traditional kimonos. Whilst a formal restaurant Zakuro's quiet, relaxed atmosphere can suit both business entertaining and more casual visitors.

The menu is available in English and this combined with the fact the staff cook the shabu-shabu / sukiyaki at the table for you mean this is an excellent place to experience this traditional food.

Usually diners all choose the same food shabu-shabu or sukiyaki and share the meal. Unusually this time we had one portion of each to share, and the restaurant were happy to go along with this slightly unusual request. The recommended menu is standard shabu-shabu (A4 rank) costing 7,500 yen, if you go for sukiyaki the cost is 8,500 yen for the food alone. After the meat and vegetables you will be offered either rice or noodles as part of the meal. The udon noodles in sukiyaki sauce are perfect.

The restaurant is located indoors, on 2F of the restaurant area of Biz Tower.
Directions: Take the Chiyoda line to Akasaka Metro Station, take Exit 3a/3b towards Akasaka Biz Tower take the escalators to 2F and you will see Zakuro ahead on your right.
Address: Zakuro (ざくろ 赤坂店), Akasaka Biz Tower 2F, Akasaka 5-3-1. Tel: +81 (0)3 3582-6841.

Open seven days a week (you need to book):	
Lunch	11.30 – 15.00
Dinner	17.00 – 10.30
Accept credit cards. Great for business meals.	

Zakuro
Akasaka

Zakuro
Akasaka

Shabu-shabu
Zakuro

Sukiyaki
Zakuro

Teppanyaki
鉄板焼き
Ginza Okahan Honten
銀座 岡半本店

Teppanyaki 鉄板焼き
Background

Teppanyaki literally means iron plate (i.e. teppan) grilled/broiled/pan-fried (i.e. yaki). It is now used to refer to a style of Japanese cuisine that uses an iron griddle to cook food, typically it refers to steak and shrimp. Note there are other Japanese cuisines that also use the griddle such as okonomiyaki and yakisoba.

Teppanyaki is a relatively modern invention dating from 1945, though it is still quintessentially Japanese. The restaurant Misono in Kobe claims to be the first to pan griddle steaks in Japan. However this most modern dish is believed to trace its roots to Genghis Khan. Legend has it that Genghis Khan invented it to prevent his food being over-cooked on open fires and first used a soldier's helmet. This technique was spread by the Mongols all over Asia, but with the fall of the Mongolian Empire it fell out of popularity. It is believed that this technique came to Sapporo where it survived in early eating establishments where customers grilled meat on top of helmet-like pots over burning coal.

At first when Misono started cooking "western influenced food" on a teppan it was more popular with foreigners. Even today teppanyaki is one of the most accessible of Japanese cuisines and is popular with visitors and for business meals. Typically a chef cooks the teppanyaki in front of the clients.

Teppanyaki, at its simplest, consists of beef followed by some vegetables and the fried rice cooked on the teppan, usually using soybean oil. At formal meals a course of abalone and/or shrimp is often included.

The key to excellent teppanyaki is the ingredients in particular the beef. The best teppanyaki uses wagyu beef either Kobe or Matsuzaka and the beef is so tender it melts in your mouth. Note: high grade beef teppanyaki is amongst the most expensive meals one can have in Japan.

Japanese Beef Sandai Wagyu

Japan has a unique history with beef, while renown today for the best beef in the world for much of the country's history beef eating was discouraged or even banned. Originally cattle were used as beasts of burden in the rice paddies and are thought to have been introduced into Japan in the 2nd century from Korea. However the growth of Buddhism discouraged the eating of meat and by 675 Emperor Temmu banned eating of it. The ban on eating four legged animals was reinforced with the introduction of the seclusion laws in 1635, effectively closing Japan to western influences. The ban lasted for over 1000 years and was only lifted in with the Meiji restoration in 1868.

In its isolation Japanese breeding and husbandry produced a distinctive herd, called Wagyu (wa means "Japanese" and gyu means "cow"). Wagyu began to be treated differently in each of the different isolated areas with things like massaging or adding beer/sake to their feed. It is not known how this first started though it is thought that it might have originally been done to improve digestion and increase hunger during the humid season, and massaging may have been done to prevent muscle cramping that may occurred due to lack of exercise on Japan's small farms. Wagyu are now genetically predisposed to produce marbled meat with a high percentage of unsaturated versus saturated fats. The resulting marbling is what gives wagyu its unique juiciness and flavour, and has resulted in it being the most prized beef in the world.

There are five major wagyu breeds: Japanese Black, Japanese Brown, Japanese Polled, Japanese Shorthorn, and Kumamoto Reds. In addition there are three famous names (based on where the cattle come from) known as "Sandai Wagyu", "the three big beefs"): Matsuzaka beef, Kobe beef and Omi beef. Whilst Kobe beef is better known in the West, in Japan Matsuzaka beef (松阪牛) is as highly prized.

Matsuzaka beef is Japanese Black beef originating from Matsuzaka. Only female wagyu are raised. The wagyu are fed plenty of fodder, soy pulp (a by-product of tofu) and ground wheat; plus they are fed beer to stimulate their eating, massaged with straw brushes, are sprayed with shochu (a weak Japanese spirit) and are taken for daily afternoon walks. This produces beef that is magical to taste.

Ginza
Okahan Honten

Ginza Okahan Honten

Ginza Okahan
Honten

Ginza Okahan Honten
8F, Ginza Kanetanaka Building, 7-6-16 Ginza
Tel +81 (0)3 3571 1417

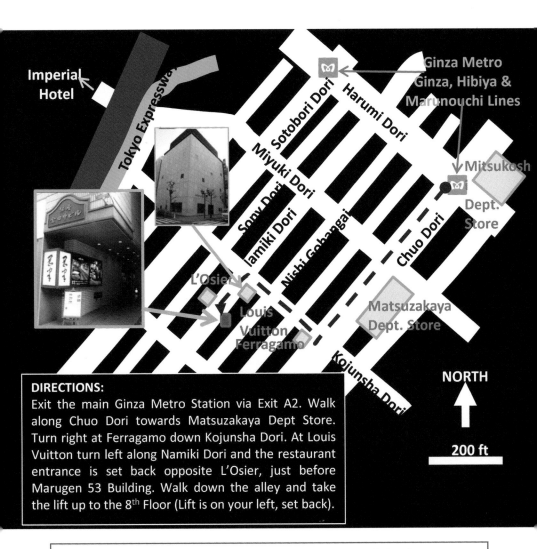

DIRECTIONS:
Exit the main Ginza Metro Station via Exit A2. Walk along Chuo Dori towards Matsuzakaya Dept Store. Turn right at Ferragamo down Kojunsha Dori. At Louis Vuitton turn left along Namiki Dori and the restaurant entrance is set back opposite L'Osier, just before Marugen 53 Building. Walk down the alley and take the lift up to the 8th Floor (Lift is on your left, set back).

Open six days a week (closed on Sunday and Public Holidays)

Lunch:	11.30-14.00 (Last Orders 13.30)
Dinner:	17.30-22.00 (Last Orders 21.30)

Teppanyaki at Ginza Okahan Honten Background and Recommended Menu

Teppanyaki is the classic meal for business entertaining. In Tokyo the historic centre for business entertaining is Ginza. The recommended restaurant Ginza Okahan Honten combines both. Located in the heart Ginza on Namiki Dori, Ginza Okahan Honten is a great example of both a teppanyaki restaurant and of Ginza upscale restaurant.

Ginza is renown as the luxury centre of Tokyo, with all the major luxury brands located either on the main roads of Chuo Dori and Harumi Dori or on Namiki Dori. In addition Namiki Dori and the surrounding roads have huge numbers of restaurants, traditional hostess bars and clubs frequented by salary men, corporate executives as well as celebrities and important politicians. Often these establishments are on the upper floors of the narrow eight storey tall buildings that line the roads. Generally these places are very expensive, though teppanyki restaurants can be much better value at lunchtime.

Ginza Okahan Honten is discreetly located on the 7th and 8th floors of a small office block, the décor is simple and the service excellent. The 7th floor serves Matsuzaka sukiyaki (very expensive but wonderful) and the 8th Floor serves teppanyaki (note: for teppanyaki take the lift to the 8th floor). Suitable for either lunch or evening dinner I have recommended a set lunch. If going in the evening it is important to book and note the cost will be significantly more expensive. The recommended meal is the foie gras teppanyaki beef set menu, it costs 6,500 yen, though not Matsuzaka beef it is still exceptional to taste. If you wish to experience Matsuzaka beef it is an extra 5,500 yen. Sit at the counter and your meal will be cooked in front of you.

Foie Gras
Ginza Okahan Honten

Sandai Wagyu
Ginza Okahan Honten

Teppanyaki
Ginza Okahan Honten

Teppanyaki
Ginza Okahan Honten

Garlic Rice
Ginza Okahan Honten

Katsu-kare
カツカレー
Grill Swiss

Katsu Kare/ Japanese Curry カレー
Background

Curry was introduced to Japan by the British Navy during the Meiji era (1869–1913). The British Navy's version was essentially a stew mixed with curry powder. This was adapted by the Imperial Japanese Navy and forms the basis of Japanese curry; it is very different than Indian-style curry. Since the 1960s it has been popular and is now so widely eaten that is one of the most popular dishes in Japan.

Japanese curry (カレー, kare) is typically available in two main forms: curry rice (カレーライス, kare raisu) and kare udon (thick noodles). The sauce is typically thick, creamy and relatively mild. The sauce is often cooked for a long time and includes a onions, carrots, and potatoes as well as meat. The type of meat often varies per region; in the Kansai beef curry is most common, while in the Kanto pork curry is most common. One of the most popular is Katsu-kare which is a breaded deep-fried pork cutlet with curry sauce.

Japanese curry rice is served in either a flat plate or a soup bowl and is eaten with a spoon. The curry sauce is poured over Japanese sticky rice and is usually served garnished with vegetables pickled in vinegar such as Fukujinzuke*. Many establishments will also serve a small salad or mound of shredded raw cabbage.

---

* Fukujinzuke is a brown crunchy pickle and is chopped up vegetables pickled and mixed with soy sauce (tends to include daikon, eggplant, lotus root and cucumber).

Grill Swiss
Ginza

Grill Swiss
Ginza

Grill Swiss,
3-5-16 Ginza, Chuo-ku
Tel: +81(0)3 3563 3206

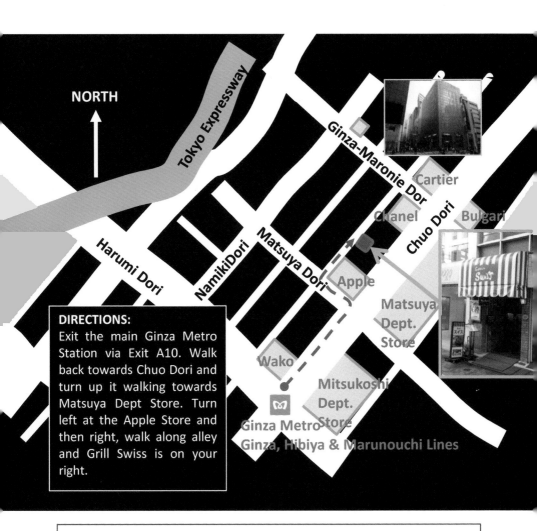

NORTH

Tokyo Expressway

Ginza-Maronie Dori

Cartier

Chanel

Chuo Dori

Bulgari

Harumi Dori

NamikiDori

Matsuya Dori

Apple

Matsuya
Dept.
Store

Wako

Mitsukoshi
Dept.
Store

Ginza Metro
Ginza, Hibiya & Marunouchi Lines

DIRECTIONS:
Exit the main Ginza Metro Station via Exit A10. Walk back towards Chuo Dori and turn up it walking towards Matsuya Dept Store. Turn left at the Apple Store and then right, walk along alley and Grill Swiss is on your right.

Open six days a week: Reservations recommended

Monday – Friday (closed Tuesday)	Lunch	11.00-15.00
	Dinner	17.00-21.00
Saturday, Sunday and Holidays		11.00-21.00

Menu is available in English.
http://rp.gnavi.co.jp/5838842/

Grill Swiss, Ginza
Background and Recommended Menu

Grill Swiss was established in 1947 and is the birthplace of "Katsu Kare". It is here that katsu (deep fried meat, usually pork or chicken, coated in egg and breadcrumbs) was first combined with curry, at the request of a famous baseball player Chiba-san, to make this ultimate simple comfort food. This dish is known as "Chiba-san's Katsu Kare".

Swiss Grill is a small unassuming place located in the heart of Ginza on Suzuran Street, a small street that runs parallel to Chuo Dori, close to Chanel and Cartier. Its décor is simple and humble, and the meals quick and reliable. Grill Swiss is typical of many small neighbourhood restaurants stuck in a time warp but providing reliable and loved food. This is not a place for business entertaining but rather a place to experience real Japan and the historic birthplace of a now national dish, Katsu Kare.

Menu options are limited. It is recommended that you chose the historic Chiba-san's Katsu Kare. Whilst the menu is in Japanese this can simply be ordered by pointing to the section of the menu featuring Chiba-san's face (see inset picture). Meal costs 1,340 yen and includes a cup of mushroom soup.

Meal time will be quick here typically 30 minutes with no fuss. Note Katsu curry is traditionally eaten with a spoon not chopsticks.

Payment is at the payment counter as you leave.

Katsu Kare
Grill Swiss

The Epilogue

Epilogue

Visiting Japan is without doubt one of the experiences of a lifetime for any food lover. It has one of the most amazing food cultures in the world and Tokyo is now recognized as one of the gourmet capitals of the world. In fact Tokyo has more Michelin stars than any other city in the world. No trip to Japan would be complete without experiencing traditional Japanese food.

Food in Japan is as much a visual feast as a mouthwatering treat, with the preparation of the meal being an art form in itself. The ingredients also play a very central role in Japanese cuisine – much of the food is essentially very simple and based on amazing ingredients cooked to perfection.

I hope this book has shown Japanese food is so much more than just sushi and fish. Whilst this guide has focused on traditional Japanese dishes and in particular on dishes connected to Tokyo, you can easily find exceptional quality modern Japanese and western cuisines.

One of the recurring themes that came up when researching this book is that many of the dishes are prepared slightly differently in Kanto versus Kansai. For example: In Tokyo eels are traditionally opened through the back, unlike Kansai where they are opened though the belly. There some famous dishes like okonomiyaki (a grilled savoury pancake) that have been omitted as they are from Kansai rather than Kanto. If you are staying longer then a trip to Osaka is a must, as this is a city famous for food.

Finally if you fancy having a beer (a very traditional activity after work in Japan) there are many places to enjoy a draft, however I recommend the Ginza Lion Bar on Chuo Dori (near the Swatch Building). The Ginza Lion Bar is one of the oldest beer bars in Tokyo, dating from the early 1900s. It is decorated in a German beer hall style and the inside is covered in mosaics. It serves Sapporo draft beer and typical Japanese bar snacks. You can get both pale and dark beers, in fact they also sell a mixed version which very surprisingly is good also. The bar is open from 11.30 to 23.00 (Monday to Saturday) and from 11.30 to 22.30 on Sundays and holidays.

Whatever food or drink you try on your trip to Tokyo it will be memorable and high quality – I hope you enjoy your time as much as I have.

About the Author

Tagore Ramoutar has spent over 16 years travelling on business around the world. He would often stay in the same city for over a week or repeatedly visit the same city. He found that after he had been brought out for a couple of business meals, there was always a few spare evenings during which he could either eat in the hotel or explore the local area. This guide is inspired by the joys of exploring the local traditional foods of various cities he has visited. In particular this book is dedicated to the team Tagore worked with and socialised with for the three years he spent travelling intensively to Japan – Thank you.

Lightning Source UK Ltd.
Milton Keynes UK
UKIC010607050713
213298UK00002B

* 9 7 8 1 9 0 7 8 3 7 3 7 1 *